Praise for Aruosa Osemwegie's
Nothing Succeeds like Excess

"If you truly want to improve your life, read this book!"
– John P. Foppe; born-without-hands Expert in Maximizing Human Capital, Advisor, Speaker and Author of *What's your Excuse? Making the most of what you have*

"Aruosa Osemwegie has the unusual ability to decode the needs of the younger generation today. No wonder his writings proffer solutions that are generated to bring results. "*Nothing Succeeds like Excess*" will launch the reader out of the realm of average onto new levels of excellence."
– Sam Adeyemi; President Success Power International and Senior Pastor Daystar Christian Centre

"This book leaves the reader with renewed confidence to do so much more. It has been carefully crafted to revive the youth in its reader. It speaks invaluable wisdom, and challenges some widely-held beliefs about the word "excess". I recommend this book to every youth – and youth-at-heart – for its timeless insight."
– Fola Adeola mni, OFR; Vice Presidential aspirant, Founding CEO Guaranty Trust Bank

"Indeed nothing succeeds like excess. To succeed in this world that is characterized by competition and dynamism, one must possess excess of whatever that is required. That is, one must be the best among the best. All qualities must be in abundance for one to excel and make meaningful impact on humanity. This book is therefore aimed at encouraging the youth to be extraordinary as that is what makes the difference. It is motivational as well as inspirational and therefore a must read for every youth who desires to stand out."

- Dr. Cosmas Maduka, President/CEO, Coscharis Group

"An inspiring book, which not only motivates you but empowers you to think big but start small, think outside the box, become creative, become innovative, hit the ground running and Do Something !!! I highly recommend this book to anyone who wants to become known as a changemaker !!!

- Nnaemeka Ikegwuonu; Executive Director, The Smallholders Foundation, Ashoka Fellow, Rolex Laureate, WISE Laureate and 2011 Future Awards Nigeria "Young Person of the Year"

"Aruosa introduced me to the radical concept of why EXCESS is good, desirable and necessary... One is never too old to learn new things and my total support goes to those wise enough to buy and read this book, for if they do so with an inquisitive and open mind, I can assure them their lives will never be the same again."

- Tonye P. Cole; CEO, Sahara Group Ltd and Convener, The Nehemiah project

"In this book, Aruosa has set down some of the rules of the game of life. He has expressed some breakthrough ideas that are a direct product of his own experiences and of others who have succeeded in the game. *Nothing Succeeds like Excess* are new thoughts . . . it's worth a read."

- Poju Oyemade; Senior Pastor Covenant Christian Centre and Convener, The Platform Nigeria

Nothing
succeeds
Like Excess
A New Code for Maximized Living

Aruosa Osemwegie
author of impact-making *Getting a Job is a Job*

for Ages
10 - 40 only

THE AUTHOR

Aruosa Osemwegie is a Human Resource consultant, Life & Career Coach, Job Search Strategist, Service Excellence Advocate and Youth Instigator. He is certified as a Senior Professional in Human Resources (SPHR) and a Global Professional in Human Resources (GPHR), with experience as a Practitioner, Consultant and Theorist in People Management. He has had learning experience at the Obafemi Awolowo University, the Lagos Business School and the Harvard Business School. He has had rich experience working and consulting in some of Nigeria's leading-light organisations. Aruosa has a particular passion for helping people 'extend themselves beyond themselves'. He is the author of the impact-making *Getting a Job is a Job: A No-Nonsense Practical Guide to Getting Your Desired Job.* His international base is in Lagos-Nigeria and his resolve with this book is to 'enable exceptional expressions' in and through the African youth.

Published by Getting a Job is a Job Resources Ltd, Lagos-Nigeria: +234 807 413 2620; info@gettingajobisajob.com

ISBN-10: 9789315325
ISBN-13: 978-9789315321

Illustrations: Gabriel Olonisakin
Cover and Interior design: Ariyo Olasunkanmi

International purchase available from www.amazon.com and other leading book retailers.

FOREWORD

My motto in life is that you are abled by your abilities and not disabled by your disabilities.

I've always believed that if you work hard and put your mind to it you will achieve great things. My ambition and drive was instilled in me from a young age. I have strong memories of my mother encouraging my brother, sister and me to go for what we want in life which gave me the confidence later in life to live my dreams.

This book reflects me in many ways. It doesn't matter who you are or where you are from, if you trust in God and yourself, you will succeed.

If you have an ambition, if you reach for the stars, as long as you are putting in hard work and living in a way that you believe merits respect, you have already achieved success.

I hope this book inspires you to achieve success no matter how big or small...

Oscar Pistorius
(The fastest man on no legs)

FIRST WORDS

In a lot of ways I see this book as a prequel to my first book, *Getting a Job is a Job: A No-Nonsense Practical Guide to Getting Your Desired Job.*

In approaching this book, I must warn you ahead; I didn't attempt to be 'politically correct' or to be 'balanced' as some may like it. I simply saw my task as that of enabling people to maximize their lives. Since each of us has just one life, since we cannot live as though we have a spare in the bank, I therefore felt that the goal before me was too precious to be tiptoed around or toyed with. As you read, please remember that I wrote with only that singularity of focus/purpose.

With that you would notice my preference for a conversational/informal style as against adhering to the strictures of grammar. My strong opinion as a writer has always been to capture and sustain the reader's interest through page by page of interesting, sometimes humorous, poignant prose – for what is a well written book that isn't read through? So I start sentences easily with 'and' and 'but' and I end some with prepositions. It wasn't my intention to wield a 'poetic license' and as such I crave the forgiveness of sticklers to the rule.

When I am able, with God's mighty assistance, to enable exceptional expressions through your life, then this book has been worth my life - and yours.

Aruosa Osemwegie
aruosa@gettingajobisajob.com

Excess	*noun* – an amount which is more than acceptable expected or reasonable. *adj* – extra
Excesses	*plural noun* – actions far beyond the limit of what is acceptable.
Excessive/Excess	*synonyms* - overkill, surplus, extra, extreme, too much, unnecessary, undue, enormous, gigantic, colossal, mammoth, giant, weighty, heavy duty, great, farthest, furthest, outermost, intense, immense, zealous, radical, fanatical.
Excess *	*noun* – a consciousness, a willingness to think and execute ideas in a quality and amount that is beyond what is presently acceptable, expected or reasonable.

---

* Our definition

Meet a young African that is on *Excess drive*...

He was born to African parents. He is a world champion sprinter who has broken his own world record some 30 times. He is referred to as the world's "fastest man on no legs". A fierce advocate of Life Without Limitations. This young man has taken the International Association of Athletics Federations (IAAF) to court and defeated them. At the 2011 World Championships, he made history as the first amputee (*yes, amputee*) to win an able-bodied world track medal. He also made history at the 2012 London Olympics as the first amputee to run with able-bodied athletes. In 2008, at age 23 he was listed on the 2008 TIME 100, making him one of the hundred most influential people in the world (a list which includes leaders, thinkers, heroes, artists, scientists and more).

He is Oscar Leonard Carl Pistorius. A South African born on 22 November 1986, known as the "Blade Runner", has a double amputation, is the world record holder in the 100, 200 and 400 metres (disability sport class T44) events and runs with the aid of carbon fibre limbs. Shortly after his birth, it was discovered that Oscar was born without the fibula (the outer and narrower of two bones of the lower leg) in both legs. When no alternative could be found, his devastated parents agreed to have their son's boneless lower limbs amputated. This *'misfortune'* has never deterred Pistorius. Instead, it has equipped him with a determination that knows no limits. He doesn't have a shred of self-pity and he instantaneously rejects any pity displayed towards him. This is because he does not regard himself otherwise. He is just as able and capable as other *'able-bodied'* folk. While in school, he ardently participated in many sporting activities, including tennis, cricket, water polo and his favourite, rugby. He had prosthetic legs, which enabled him to participate in sports. He later had running prosthetics made for him.

In June 2003, Pistorius seriously injured one of his knees while playing rugby. He was sent to the High Performance Centre at the University of Pretoria to undergo a rehabilitation programme. While there he proceeded to train tirelessly towards his recovery, under the watchful eyes of Coach Ampie Louw. The recovery programme included some athletic activity on the track. At school he was not as enthusiastic about athletics as he was about other sports, but while at the rehabilitation centre, he changed his mind about athletics. He started running in January 2004 and by March 2004 was competing in athletics meetings. Within eight months, Oscar was competing with the best in the world at the Athens September 2004 Paralympics. His courage, persistence and optimism were illustrated at that Paralympics in the 200m semi-final. There were two false starts to the race, and during the third attempt, Pistorius was shockingly left behind in his blocks. He watched as the field sped away. Not one to give up, he lifted himself off the blocks and proceeded to rocket past his fellow contenders, winning the race and breaking the record for double amputees. The next day, Pistorius gave another astonishing performance by winning the final and breaking his own record from the previous day, becoming the first amputee to ever run the 200m in under 22 seconds.

In 2007, Pistorius took part in his first international competitions for able-bodied athletes. However, his artificial lower legs, while enabling him to compete, generated claims that he had an unfair advantage over able-bodied runners. The same year, the International Association of Athletics Federations (IAAF) amended its competition rules to ban the use of "any technical device that incorporates springs, wheels or any other element that provides a user with an advantage over another athlete not using such a device". It claimed that the amendment was not specifically aimed at Pistorius. After monitoring his track performances and carrying out tests, scientists took the view that Pistorius enjoyed considerable advantages over athletes without prosthetic limbs. On the strength of these findings, on 14 January 2008 the IAAF ruled him ineligible for competitions conducted under its rules, including the 2008 Summer Olympics.

Pistorius called the decision "premature and highly subjective" and pledged to continue fighting for his dream. In February 2008, he employed the services of law firm Dewey & LeBoeuf to challenge the ruling via an appeal and later that month, travelled to America to take part in a series of further tests carried out at Rice University in Houston by a team of scientists including Hugh Herr, Ph.D. and Rodger Kram, Ph.D. Pistorius subsequently appealed against the adverse decision to the Court of Arbitration for Sport (CAS) in Lausanne, Switzerland, and appeared before the tribunal at the end of April 2008. After a two-day hearing, on 16 May 2008, the Court of Arbitration for Sport upheld Oscar's appeal and the IAAF council decision was revoked with immediate effect. The CAS panel unanimously determined that Dr. Brüggemann (the doctor that conducted initial tests on him) only tested Oscar's biomechanics at full-speed when he was running in a straight line (unlike a real 400m race), that the report did not consider the disadvantages that Oscar suffers at the start and acceleration phases of the race, and that overall there was no evidence that Oscar had any net advantage over able-bodied athletes. In response to the announcement, Pistorius said: "My focus throughout this appeal has been to ensure that disabled athletes be given the chance to compete and compete fairly with able-bodied athletes. I look forward to continuing my quest to qualify for the Olympics."

Although eligible to compete in the 2008 Summer Olympic Games in Beijing, Pistorius did not qualify for the South African team. Despite achieving third place and a personal best time of 46.25 seconds in the 400 metres in Lucerne, Switzerland, on 16 July 2008, this was short of the Olympic qualification time of 45.55 seconds. Undeterred, at the 2008 Summer Paralympics, he took the gold medals in the 100, 200 and 400 metres (T44) sprints. Then later on July 19, 2011, with a time of 45.07 in 400m, he achieved the "A" qualifying standard for the able-bodied 2011 World Championships and 2012 Olympics. He participated in the 400m sprint and 4x400m relay, but was eliminated in the semi-final of the 400m sprint (finishing last with a time of 46.19secs). Though he wasn't selected for the final 4x400m relay event but being part of South Africa's relay team, he made history as the first amputee to win an able-bodied world track medal because his team won the silver medal. In the middle of all of this, he is studying for a Bachelor of Commerce (B.Com.) at the University of Pretoria.

"You're not disabled by the disabilities you have but you are able by the abilities you have" – Oscar Pristorius.

"It was only recently that living with prosthetic legs was seen as a huge impediment, but he has turned this perception upside down. He's on the cusp of a paradigm shift in which disability becomes ability, disadvantage becomes advantage. Yet we mustn't lose sight of what makes an athlete great. It's too easy to credit Pistorius' success to technology. Through birth or circumstances, some are given certain gifts, the hours devoted to training, the desire to be the best, that is at the true heart of a champion"- www.time.com

To my parents
Semmy & Maggy

BOOK @ A GLANCE

END

Introduction

Introduction

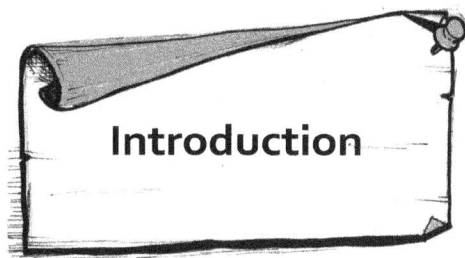

On the 10th day of May 1994 the people of South Africa cried, "Free at last", signifying/indicating their final freedom from the repressive inhuman apartheid as Nelson Mandela was sworn in as the first black President. In a different fashion, many years earlier, on Oct 1st of 1960, Nigeria had also gotten her *'freedom'* from colonial rule.

However, the African youth has never truly been free. Daily, the freedom of choice and expression, which is the highest freedom there is, is repressed and trampled upon – and this sums up the story of the Nigerian youth. "Weep not Child" wouldn't be a good refrain for me now as my heart truly bleeds for us young people. I am "no longer at ease" as I recall Myles Munroe's assertion that the graveyards bear

INCAPACITATED YOUTH

the richest deposits – deposits of unsung songs, unwritten writers, presidents that presided over no one, un-invented inventions, undiscovered discoveries, etc

But enough is enough!

What we couldn't achieve as a nation on the 1ˢᵗ of Oct 1960 is what this book sets out to do – to set young people free...truly free to live their dreams...truly free to choose and express themselves...expressing themselves maximally.

Your dream must come alive. Your vision must be birthed. Yes I know. I know that helplessness and hopelessness pervades the air. It is no longer news that "there are no jobs". Neither is it news that "there is no capital to do business". Even children now know that our leaders are corrupt and insensitive. There have even been poverty-induced riot in London, Greece and some part of Europe. The question, still unanswered, in the hearts and minds of young people is this, "What can I do"? I told you . . . it's hopelessness and helplessness. Many have concluded that there is nothing that they can do. They have decided to do only one thing – NOTHING! Because that is all that they can clearly see and easily do. Some have decided to simply lie dead. A large majority have already made the decision to live a moderate life – accepting whatever comes, however it comes, whenever it comes, from whomever it comes, anyhow it comes. No wonder one said the other day that a lot of us live our lives in "quiet desperation".

Moderation is fatal, moderation is akin to extinction. Again I remember the rich graveyards . . . the world wouldn't even know that you came. Of one it was said "she came, she saw and she conquered". Of another, all that was said was, "he came. . . Moderation is truly a fatal thing, whereas nothing succeeds like excess. Not a thing succeeds like excess. In this book, I bring you a hidden code for maximized living, an already existing code that stares us in the face, but we have long ignored it. **Thinking and doing at the level that is currently acceptable or proper is the very key to dying unfulfilled and unmaximized.** But I bring you a new code for living at your most – you could call this the **code for true freedom**.

The helplessness to which many have become enslaved/imprisoned is daily being worsened by feelings of hopelessness – hope has lost its audacity! There are at least two reasons for this. As young people consider the present crop of corrupt and insensitive leadership, they look to the future with hopelessness. In essence, bad it is how bad today is, but worse it is when tomorrow doesn't seem to bear the change hoped for. The last strands of hope that young people have has been annulled and postponed several times. Annulled and deferred by the actions of a few and by statements such as "there is time for everything". . . "take it easy". . ."wait for your time" and other well-worn statements that seem to teach that, 1) today is a day to do nothing; 2) wait for the future; 3) there is a sequence that must be followed; and 4) just wait and everything would be fine. **The future has thus become our biggest excuse! Gosh**!!! Wait for what? Still we have waited . . . and waited . . . and . . . waited – and nothing has changed. Didn't Albert Einstein (*Physicist, 1879-1955*) say that *"Insanity is doing the same thing over and over again and expecting different results"*? We obviously require new thoughtware – a changed mindset, a new (not a refurbished) approach. I guess that is why Albert Einstein also made the point that, *"we cannot solve our problems with the same thinking we used when we created them".*

Ladies and gentlemen, today, due to all the above, Youth stands imprisoned! True freedom, the freedom to choose and to express self is imprisoned. Young people, male and female, in different corners of Africa, sit amidst helplessness/hopelessness, waiting for the future which the older generation speak of . . . waiting, either doing nothing or more likely doing little. Very likely sitting in fear, immobile in thought and deed. Many more are mobile, deploying less of their best selves – small efforts, mediocre attempts, little courage, cut-to-size dreams, daring little, risking nothing, stretching little, armed with excuses, making little contribution, focused on self, . . . the list goes on and on.

Whereas, we all need to throw ourselves upon this generation with the full weight of all the gifts and possibilities that God has placed IN us and AROUND us. **Excess must become our core value.** If the greatness IN us must come alive, if the greatness AROUND us must come alive, we cannot afford little ideas, small plans, small efforts and small impact in small communities....no, no no. It is too late for smallness, we have just one life to live. The large-sized post-independence challenges faced by Africans cannot even be solved by small thinking. The society has gotten tired of all manner of small-hearted attempts . . . half-hearted . . . lame attempts to bring about long lasting development.

Today a new chapter unfolds - it is *Excess*. Today is the day of More! If we are to live a truly maximized life, then we have to be and do at a level or amount that is more than what is presently acceptable, expected or reasonable. What we need are dreams, thoughts and actions far beyond the limits of what is currently acceptable. This is the day of the UNREASONABLE. This is the message of this book. This is the revolution! Arise and shine for your light is finally come.

Chapter One

It is late for smallness!

It is late for smallness!

It is very late for smallness. It is totally late for moderate thinking, moderate visions, moderate efforts, moderate impact, moderate value etc. It is certainly much too late for you and me to be moderate, modest, average, normal, mediocre, toned down, played down, regular, reasonable, or restrained. The reason is so obvious it doesn't even need telling. I would imagine that if you approach a forest to hunt rabbits, a bow and arrow may even be an over-kill. But if you prepare to pounce on a forest full of wolves and lions, there are a lot of people who would consider it a streak of insanity if you *'armed'* yourself with a spanner! What is my point exactly?

As at the time of this writing, Nigeria has turned 50 and she still grapples with basic developmental challenges. Don't get me wrong. On a good day, I am

not one to paint a picture of doom and gloom. All through these 50 years we have sought for selfless leaders. Instead what did we get? Insensitive, corrupt and visionless leadership. We had hoped for followers who would understand and appreciate that the real government is the people. Instead what did we get? A mass of people ready to sell their conscience to the highest bidder. There are of course those who argue that "the people get the leadership that it deserves".

In addition to poor leadership, 70% of the people live below the poverty line of $1.25 (less than N200) per day[a]. This means that 7 out of every 10 Nigerians have less than the amount of money required to meet basic needs (gosh! I hope this isn't true). There is poor or insufficient infrastructure – the lack of electricity has become our expectation. The industries are producing nowhere near their installed capacity and that is for those that haven't been shut down already. Unemployment rate is high – a large percentage of the productive workforce (largely made up of youth) is unemployed or underemployed or more importantly, don't-see-any-possibility-of-being-employed. No one is providing capital to start-ups, leaving many entrepreneurial dreams as mere dreams. With lending rates going in only one direction...up!!! All this is happening at a time when the world has been humbled by a financial crisis. This means even the

w o r l d   c a n   o n l y   h e l p   l i t t l e .
My point is . . . gigantic challenges require gigantic
solutions...massiveness...excess! This isn't a
rehearsal, this is the real deal! You don't confront a
fully armed Goliath with a catapult – only a youth
like David would dare though!

Again I say to you friend that it is late for smallness.
Youth stands incarcerated by the hopelessness and
helplessness being peddled around town. The
ultimate freedom (the freedom of choice and
expression) is starving under lock and key, without
air and with a death sentence over its head. Except ...
except you and I do something. Except you and I do
something NOW! This book is doing something
about it and it is doing it one reader at a time. So how
come the young feel hopeless and helpless? Little
wonder that one wrote the other day that being
hopeful is audacious...being hopeful takes boldness
... confidence...courage! When they say "there are no
jobs" the young feel helpless and hope ebbs away.
When the young hear that "there is no capital" for
starting businesses, his shoulder drops, his
confidence wanes. Add to this equation, the
prevalence of award-winning corruption amongst
political and business leaders and what do you get?

No Jobs + No Start-Up Capital + Corrupt Leaders =
Bleak-Hopeless-Helpless-Incapacitated Youth

No Jobs + No Start-Up Capital + Corrupt Leaders =
No Hope-No Help-Immobilised Youth

To set at liberty them that are oppressed or imprisoned would require massive, no-holds-barred thinking and efforts – Excess!

The Prevailing Code

To make the situation worse, the prevailing code can be summed up in one word – Wait. To quadruple the challenge, for so long the young have been told to wait. Don't ask me, "wait for what"? We have commonly been told to "wait for your time"; "there is a time for everything"; "this is how things are done" etc. All of these point to two things, specifically 2 things: Timing and Sequence.

- **Timing.** It is true that there is a time for everything – a time to be born and a time to die. Does that mean that now is not the time? Or does the statement indicate that the future automatically holds perfect timing? It is a fallacy to claim or suggest that as long as you are a young person then you don't have to place both of your hands firmly around opportunities that you see around you. And it is even cruel to suggest or imply that a youth has no business maximizing his/her talents today. This is what Wayne Dyer (*self-help advocate, author, 1940 –date*) had to say, *"Go for it now. The future is promised to no one."*

- **Sequence.** We have been told that there is an established order of things. Let me give you an example please: birth – toddler – adolescent –

teenager –adult. Or this one: crèche – playgroup – nursery – primary – secondary – JAMB – university/polytechnic – NYSC – office work or Masters or marriage. Maybe you would prefer this example: employee – retire at 50 – employer @ 51. So if you want to be successful follow the tradition. Right? Very wrong. Find your own rhythm – create your own sequence.

The future has become our greatest excuse.
So what is the fuss about timing and sequence? Youths have believed this lie and are now lethargic – doing nothing or doing too little. This is the evil I see under the sun!!! Lackluster youths . . . young people who have subscribed to modest visions, mediocre efforts and regular impact. Youth has become a synonym for delayed or deflated greatness. We obviously cannot debunk these well-spun lies using kid gloves. It is late for smallness like I said. We have to act excessively – our very best thoughts and efforts poured out NOW! Our most daring actions NOW!

> *Trust no future, howe'er pleasant!*
> *Let the dead past bury its dead!*
> *Act, - act in the living Present!*
> *Heart within and God o'erhead.*

- Henry Wadsworth Longfellow, *Psalm of Life*

To know if the future has become our greatest excuse

just listen to our vocabulary: "I would love to. . . "I would . . . "Someday . . . "When I grow up . . ."One day I would . . . "One of these days . . . "When I have more time . . . "In my time . . . "When I have money . . ." and so on.

"Now is the accepted time, not tomorrow, not some more convenient season. It is today that our best work can be done and not some future day or future year. It is today that we fit ourselves for the greater usefulness of tomorrow. Today is the seed time, now are the hours of work, and tomorrow comes the harvest and the playtime".

- W. E. B. Du Bois
(William Edward Burghardt Du Bois; sociologist, historian, civil rights activist, Pan-Africanist, author, and editor; the first African-American to earn a doctorate at Harvard, 1868 – 1963).

Chapter Two

**Youth or Singleness-
a badly defined brand**

Youth or Singleness -- a badly defined brand

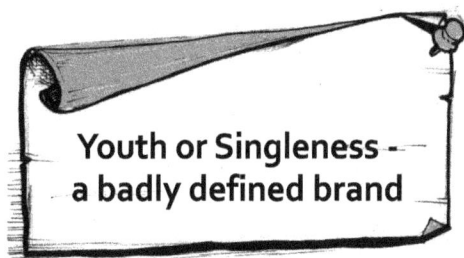

I grew up in the south-western part of Nigeria and even though I was privileged by God's grace and the unwavering commitment of my parents (Semmy and Maggy) to go to decent schools, I grew up feeling like there was something wrong with being young. It just seemed like being a boy was a bad thing in itself. I still recall my ninth birthday when bottles of Coke (or Pepsi...not sure) were arranged on the table to symbolize the number of my years. By simple, unqualified Maths, that should be nine bottles . . . right? Yeah. But I wanted 10 bottles – I was *nine years young* but I preferred being 10 years *'old'*. Fast forward to my Secondary School days . . . I was keenly interested in growing a beard as well. But why not? Only older people had beards, so I needed my own

THE DEFINING PERIOD OF OUR LIVES

UNLIVED. UNLIVED

set. And it didn't matter that I wasn't yet 14!

The above *'older quest'* depicts in a small measure the pursuit of *'older'* by the younger. Youthfulness is being lost/mortgaged or remains unopened because of a search for a better life called 'olderness'. The idea that being older is better, is the world's oldest branding campaign and maybe the most successful yet! Too many young people, all over the place, instead of appreciating, exploiting and maximizing their youthfulness or singleness are rather on a race to become or to look older. What is the result? The defining period of our lives is put on hold! Or allowed to fly past – UNLIVED. What a tragedy!

Youth or singlehood, in my opinion, would easily win the award as the worst defined brand ever. Except you and I redefine it – starting right now. The world has placed the wrong labels on youth and to compound it . . . to thoroughly compound it, ladies and gentlemen, even the youths have accepted those wrong labels. And today, youth stands condemned to mediocrity and lackluster performance. It is sad that the youth are also confused as to the label to bear. The question "who do people say I am?", must be answered without any equivocation . . . any ambiguity . . . without a stutter. The answer: "I am young, proud of it and taking my place". For if the trumpet gives an uncertain sound, who shall prepare himself/herself . . .?

What is Youth?
Youth stands imprisoned or immobilized or weakened by the following factors:
1) the wrong branding that we 'inherited';
2) the confusion as to who we are or what our place is;
3) the seeming absence of capital;
4) seeming absence of jobs;
5) inadequate knowledge or information;
6) pursuit of marriage as an end;
7) the challenge of being *'too young'*;
8) the call to *'wait for our time'* and
9) the idea that there is a rigid sequence to success and achievement.

If I have left any out, forgive me, though I reckon that the above are the worst offenders. Is young wrong? Definitely, NO!

Say this after me:

But rather, this day . . . . (fill in today's date)
I arise as a proud young .... (boy, girl, man, woman);
proud to be young;
ready to discover, deepen and deploy all the strength and ideas within me;
ready to improve, influence and impact this world right NOW!

What really is Youth?

Unknown to young people, the truth actually has a different colour and I intend to show it to you in a moment. What is common to these people:

Thomas Edison
Alexander G. Bell
Karl Benz
Federico Faggin
Ted Hoff
Stan Mazor
Masatoshi Shima
Tim Berners-Lee

These are the people who invented five of the things that have FUNDAMENTALLY changed the way we live.[a]

THE ELECTRIC LIGHT BULB: The man who made the first practical light bulb was Thomas Alva Edison.   In 1879, he invented a light bulb that burned for 40 hours. At the time a light bulb only worked for about 13 hours making it too expensive for everyone to afford. This was a very important invention because until then people only had oil lamps or candles to provide light after the sun went down. Now they could work, study or read more easily, after dark. They were more productive. This meant that they could get more work done in the same amount of time. This was also an invention that everyone wanted and could afford to buy. It was because of this that all houses began to get electricity. Before the electric light bulb most houses didn't have electricity.

THE TELEPHONE: In 1876, Alexander Graham Bell displayed his new invention to the world at the Centennial Exhibition in Philadelphia, New York. The telephone allowed people to talk to each other over long distances. It used wires and electricity to move sound from one place to another. Before the telephone you could only communicate to someone far away by writing a letter or sending a telegram. A telegram was kind of like a text message but it could only be sent to a special location where they knew how to read it. Now with the telephone, you could hear someone's voice and answer them right then. It changed the way we lived and especially the way we worked. People were able to call for help in an emergency. You could place an order to a store or call someone to say you were going to be late. Soon almost every home and business had a telephone. As time went on, other inventors found new ways to use the telephone wires. Now we have fax machines and cellular phones but it all started with the telephone.

THE AUTOMOBILE: In 1885, German engineer, Karl Benz designed and built the world's first practical automobile. There was a car in existence before this, but it ran on steam so it wasn't very easy to use and it was very expensive. Automobiles were still too expensive for most people to own.

THE MICROPROCESSOR: In 1971, a company called Intel introduced the world's first single chip microprocessor. It was invented by Federico Faggin, Ted Hoff, Masatoshi Shima and Stan Mazor, who all worked for Intel. Like the light bulb, this was an improvement on an invention that was already in existence. A microprocessor is a chip that makes up the brain of a computer. These people came up with a way to put all the parts that make up the computer's brain on one small chip. This was an important invention because now computers could be made small enough and cheap enough for many people to afford them. In addition, because the chips were so small they could be used to invent or improve all kinds of gadgets like TV's, wrist watches, cars, appliances and computer games.

THE INTERNET AND THE WORLD WIDE WEB: Many people worked to invent the internet. The United States military set up a way for computers to communicate with each other (networking) in 1969. Scientists could now work together on projects without having to be in the same place. These scientists saw how useful it was and began inventing more things to do on this network. They invented the email in 1971 and shared files and pictures easily by 1973. But until 1991 it was still just a thing that only scientists and technical people used because it was very hard to figure out.

Between 1989 and 1991 Tim Berners-Lee invented the World Wide Web (with help of course). He invented an easy-to-use way that all kinds of different computers could communicate. He did this by inventing a computer language that any computer could read, HTML (HyperText Markup Language). This is the language that is used to create web pages. He also invented a way that was easy for people to use to find information on other computers. The URL (Universal Resource Locator) is what we call a web site address. It is because of Tim Berners-Lee that we can just type in a website address (Example: www.mywebsite.com) instead of trying to remember a bunch of numbers.

INVENTION	NAME	Age @ invention
The Electric Light Bulb In 1879	Thomas Edison (1847 – 1931)	32
The Telephone In 1876	Alexander Graham Bell (1847 – 1922)	29
The automobile in 1885	Karl Benz (1844 – 1929)	41
The Microprocessor In 1971	Federico Faggin (1941 – date)	30
	Marcian Ted Hoff (1937 – date)	34
	Stan Mazor (1941 – date)	30
	Masatoshi Shima (1943 – date)	28
The World Wide Web and URL from 1989	Tim Berners-Lee (1955 – date)	24

It is instructive to note that all these people discovered/invented these generation-impacting things while in their youth. Amazing isn't it?

Ok, let me show you something else. The names below represent a cross-section of successful people who have impacted, inspired and changed our lives. Can you spot the similarity/similarities in their stories?[b]

Bill Gates
Ben Carson
David Oyedepo
Fola Adeola & Tayo Aderinokun
Ben Murray-Bruce
Mark Zuckerberg
Steve Jobs
Shawn Carter (Jay Z)
Sam Adeyemi
Henry Ford
Andrew Carnegie
Tuface Idibia
Martin Luther King Jnr
Aliko Dangote
Ali Baba (Atoyota .A. Akpobome)
Myles Munroe

Aliko Dangote. Born in 1957. He is Africa's richest individual and the 43rd richest man in the world with a worth in excess of $16.1billion (as at March 2013). His interests are in sugar, flour milling, salt processing, cement manufacturing, textiles, real estate, and oil and gas. Two of the companies that make up the Dangote group were incorporated in 1981 – Aliko was 24 years old.

Andrew Carnegie. Born in 1835. He was a business magnate, steel tycoon and philanthropist and often regarded as the second-richest man in history after John D. Rockefeller Snr. You can say that Andrew's climb to fame started in 1856 when he took out a loan from a local bank and invested $217.50 in the Woodruff Sleeping Car Company. After about two years, he began to receive a return of about $5000 annually, more than three times his salary from the railroad – he was 21 years old at the time he made the investment and was 30 when he formed his first company.

Ben Carson. Born in 1951. He is an African-American neurosurgeon and the Director of Pediatric Neurosurgery at Johns Hopkins Hospital in the US. At age 33, he became the hospital's youngest Director of Pediatric Neurosurgery. He was awarded the Presidential Medal of Freedom, the highest civilian award in the United States by President George W. Bush in 2008. Holds up to 61 honorary doctorate degrees. In 1987, Carson made medical history by being the first surgeon in the world to successfully separate twins conjoined at the back of the head – he was 36 years old.

Ben Murray-Bruce. Born in 1956. He is the Chairman, Silverbird Group – one of the largest entertainment companies in Nigeria and Africa. Consisting of diverse holdings of radio, TV, beauty pageant and movie distribution via its cinema holdings in Nigeria, Ghana, Zambia and Kenya. It is thought to be the third largest media entertainment company in Western Africa. It is reported that he started the company in 1980 with a N20,000.00 loan from family and friends – he was 24 years old at that time.

Bill Gates. Born in 1955. He is an American business magnate, philanthropist, author, and is co-chairman of Microsoft, the software company he founded with Paul Allen. He is consistently ranked among the world's wealthiest people and was the wealthiest overall from 1995 to 2009, excluding 2008, when he was ranked third – he is currently the 2nd richest man in the world. With help from billionaire buddy Warren Buffett, he has convinced nearly 60 of the world's wealthiest to sign his "Giving Pledge," promising to donate the majority of their wealth to charity either during their lifetime or after death. He founded Microsoft as a 20 year young youth; he was 23 years when Microsoft's revenues exceeded $1m and 26 years when they finally incorporated the company.

David Oyedepo. Born in 1954. He is the General Overseer of Living Faith Church (a.k.a Winners Chapel) which has branches in over 50 countries all over the world and an excess of 400 local branches in Nigeria alone. He is also the senior pastor of the acclaimed Faith Tabernacle, a 50,000 seat church auditorium reputed to be the largest church auditorium in the world by the Guinness Book of Records. Bishop Oyedepo is an author of over 60 books; the promoter of two universities (Covenant and Landmark); a secondary school (Faith Academy); a nationwide chain of primary schools (Kingdom Heritage School); and a Christian leadership training institute (Word of Faith Bible Institute). When he got the mandate to start in 1981, he was 27 years young; ordained a Bishop at 34 years and expanded into Lagos at age 35.

Fola Adeola & Tayo Aderinokun. Born in 1954 and 1955 respectively. Co-founders of Guaranty Trust Bank - which commenced operations as a commercial bank in Nigeria in 1990. GTBank, as it is called, though the third biggest, is the Most Profitable Bank in Nigeria. The bank presently has an asset base of over one trillion Naira, shareholders in excess of 190 billion naira and employs over 5,000 people in Nigeria, the Gambia, Ghana, Liberia, Sierra Leone and the United Kingdom. In 2007, the Bank entered history books as the first Nigerian financial institution to undertake a US$350 million regulation-S Eurobond issue and a US$750 million Global Depositary Receipts (GDR) Offer. The listing of the GDRs on the London Stock Exchange in July that year made the bank the first Nigerian company and African bank to be listed on the main market of the London Stock Exchange. This homegrown success was started by two men at 36 and 35 years old.

Ben Okri. Born 1959. A Nigerian poet and novelist. He has received honorary doctorate degrees from the University of Westminster (1997) and the University of Essex (2002), and was awarded an OBE (Order of the British Empire) in 2001. Since he published his first novel, *Flowers and Shadows,* Okri has risen to international acclaim, and he is often described as one of Africa's greatest writers. He has also won the Commonwealth Writers Prize for Africa, the Aga Khan Price for Fiction, and was given a Crystal Award by the World Economic Forum. He is also a Fellow of the Royal Society of Literature. He published his first novel at age 21 and was awarded the 1991 Booker Prize at age 32 for his best work yet, *The Famished Road.*

Martin Luther King Jnr. Born in 1929. He was an American clergyman, civil rights activist, and prominent leader in the African American civil rights movement. He is best known for being an iconic figure in the advancement of civil rights in the United States and around the world, using nonviolent methods following the teachings of Mahatma Gandhi. King is often presented as a heroic leader in the history of modern American liberalism. He was posthumously awarded the Presidential Medal of Freedom in 1977 and Congressional Gold Medal in 2004; and Martin Luther King, Jr. Day was established as a U.S. federal holiday in 1986. In 1964, at the age 35, King became the Youngest Person to receive the Nobel Peace Prize for his work to end racial segregation and racial discrimination through civil disobedience and other non-violent means.

Peter Drucker. Born in 1909. A Writer, Professor and Management Consultant. Often referred to as The Man who invented Management. His books, scholarly essays and popular articles explored how humans are organized across the business, government and the nonprofit sectors of society. He is one of the best-known and most widely influential thinkers and writers on the subject of management theory and practice. His writings have predicted many of the major developments of the late twentieth century, including privatization and decentralization; the rise of Japan to economic world power; the decisive importance of marketing; and the emergence of the information society with its necessity of lifelong learning. He earned a Doctorate in Public and International Law at age 22 and wrote his first best-selling book, *The End of Economic Man* in 1939 as a 30-year young man.

Shawn Carter (Jay-Z). Born in 1969. Shawn Corey Carter (stage name Jay-Z) is an American rapper and businessman. He is one of the most financially successful hip-hop artistes and entrepreneurs in America, having a net worth of over $450 million as of 2010. He has sold approximately 50 million albums worldwide, while receiving 13 Grammy Awards for his musical works, and numerous additional nominations. Jay-Z co-owns the 40/40 Club, is part-owner of the NBA's New Jersey Nets and is also the creator of the clothing line Rocawear. He is the former CEO of Def Jam Recordings, one of the three founders of Roc-A-Fella Records, and the founder of Roc Nation. As an artiste, he holds the record for most number one albums by a solo artiste on the Billboard 200. He was 27 when he released his 1996 debut album *Reasonable Doubt*.

Sam Adeyemi. Born in 1967. The President of Success Power International and Senior Pastor of Daystar Christian Centre, a fast growing, life changing church committed to "raising role models" based in Lagos. He is a dynamic Pastor, Teacher, and Motivational speaker and host of a popular radio and TV programme, *Successpower*, which airs on radio stations within and outside Nigeria. He is a much sought-after speaker by churches and the business world both nationally and internationally. He is one of the few championing the course for a "new Nigeria" and the reformation of the African continent as a whole. He has authored several books. He was 28 years when the church started.

Tuface Idibia. Born in 1975. Innocent Ujah Idibia (better known as Tuface), is currently one of the most popular artistes on the African music scene. He won the award for the 'Best African Act' in the 2005 MTV Europe Awards. In 2010, with his *Unstoppable* Album (The Intl. Edition), he won 2 awards at the

2010 Sound City Music Video Awards, also won the Channel O Most Gifted Western African and the MTV African Music Awards for the Best Male and Artist of the year, making him the most successful pop singer in Africa. He was the lead vocalist of the Sony All African '08 Project alongside seven other stars across Africa recording their first singles with R.Kelly and Prince Lee titled "Hands across the World" (it was used as Airtel's TV and radio commercial). He was 29 years old when he hit the world with his album *Face to Face* which featured the award winning track 'African Queen'.

Steve Jobs. Born in 1955. Chairman, Co-founder and CEO of Apple Inc. Jobs also previously served as chief executive of Pixar Animation Studios; he became a member of the board of directors of The Walt Disney Company in 2006, following the acquisition of Pixar by Disney. He was credited in the 1995 movie Toy Story as an executive producer. He was awarded the National Medal of Technology from President Ronald Reagan in 1984 with Steve Wozniak (among the first people to ever receive the honor). On November 27, 2007, Jobs was named the most powerful person in business by Fortune Magazine. After graduating from high school in 1972, Jobs attended Reed College in Portland, Oregon, for two years. He dropped out after one semester to visit India and study eastern religions in the summer of 1974. They raised $1,300 in start-up money by selling Jobs's microbus and Steve Wozniak's calculator. At first they sold circuit boards(the boards that hold the internal components of a computer) while they worked on the computer prototype. Apple Inc is currently the Most Valuable Company in the world and the world's Most Valuable Technology Company ahead of arch rival Microsoft.

Apple's first product was launched when Jobs was 21 years young; company incorporated when he turned 22; went public with it at 25; made $1 billion sales when he turned 27; and lost the company and left at age 30 and was only able to return at 41.

Take another look at all the people listed above. They either accomplished greatness in their youth or they started the feats/enterprises for which they are well known as young people. So I ask the question again, "What is youth?

*Y*outh is Experimentation. The inventions that have changed our lives were not always discovered by conscious, calculated efforts but by men experimenting with ideas. The unknown future is daily conquered and arrived at when people experiment with the present. The possibilities that would shape the world of tomorrow lies at the feet of experimentation. No one would ever know, if it isn't tried.

*Y*outh is Ignorance. We can all be accused of knowing a lot about what IS but less of what COULD be. An un-educated imagination may sometimes be the greatest gift from God. *"Never tell a young person that something cannot be done. God may have been waiting for centuries for somebody ignorant enough of the impossible to do that thing."* – Dr. J. A. Holmes.

*Y*outh is Strength. "The glory of the youth is their strength . . ." There are too many tasks that require just good old strength. Untiring muscles. Untiring legs and feet. There is a reason why it is said that "health is wealth". Every nation is dependent on the number of productive people that it possesses. And when the counting of productive people begins, there is an age where it stops (your guess is as good as mine).

*Y*outh is Curiosity. Too many questions. Too many quests. We should always be spurred on by this one question, "What if?" What is at the end of the tunnel? What is on top of the mountain? Why does it always move in that direction? Can't it go faster? Can't it last longer? Couldn't it be cheaper? Curiosity is the fuel of life and the engine of industry.

*Y*outh is Drive. Too many ideas would still remain on the shelves and lose their shelf life if not for drive. To bring about change, all you need is one man or woman that is DRIVEN. The force that pushes ideas forward . . . forward through forests of doubt . . . forward through inadequate resources is spelled D R I V E.

*Y*outh is Hunger/Thirst. Insatiable! Never seen a bunch that is beyond satisfying like a bunch of young people. Ever setting new goals (consciously or unconsciously). Ever in pursuit of something. Woe betide us if we wake up one day and we've lost the hunger for more.

*Y*outh is disdain for rules or order. "This is the way it is done" is the surest recipe for stagnation and backwardness. Every record is broken at some point and it is only broken by people who saw possibilities in their minds. "Isn't there another way" is breakthrough question No. 1. There was a time when the whole world agreed that the earth was flat. . . until Galileo said otherwise. There was a time in the United Kingdom when it was inconceivable for women to earn as much money and benefits as men (can you even imagine such absurdity!) . . .until some semi-skilled women stood their ground in one of Ford Motor Company plants in the United Kingdom.

*Y*outh is Creativity. Oh! the beauty of the imagination. The splendor of inspiration. Awed by the beauty of human ingenuity, *'the creator'* in each of us is awakened. Without creativity the world would have been deprived of the 'ancient seven wonders of the world'; without it the city of Dubai and its Burj Al Arab wouldn't exist.

*Y*outh is Passion. Facts are good, since information can enrich. And logic may sway. But none can beat the conviction of passion. Any day, the world would easily line up behind passion ahead of common sense. More products and services are being sold daily by passionate people. Some brands have gained a cult-like following due, in part, to the strong feelings evoked by their services, products or delivery style. Enthusiasm is contagious – spread it.

Youth is the lifeline of the world. And the future. Therefore, **Young is an advantage.**

Say this after me:

"I am young, "proud of it and taking my place".
No longer will I feel inadequate or ill-
equipped. My age is an advantage.
I am privileged to be young now, old will come
but it's not here.
Marriage will come but it's not here. I am not
waiting to 'settle' down by rushing into
marriage. Instead I will settle down now to
maximize my destiny.
I won't let this season of my life go in a breeze.
No! I will use it and squeeze it, till there is
none left.

No longer will I place my youth on 'hold'
because of the race to look or be older.
I am me and that is sufficient. I am a success
already because I am young.
I am young and every day I bring my
contribution to this world.
I will learn and learn and continue learning.
I will serve and serve and serve - for service is
the way up.
I am on Excess-drive from today for youth is
excess".

A consciousness of our youthfulness and its advantages is a consciousness that frees us from 'our deepest fear'. This consciousness liberates us to release our entire self with its unknown possibilities into the world – regardless of our circumstances. *"Success is who you are"* (Sam Adeyemi) not who is or what is around you. You are not your circumstances. Some people have done nothing with better circumstances, some little whereas some have squeezed greatness out of storms, out of poverty, out of hopelessness . . . the choice is yours. What is it going to be? Remember that you came pre-loaded. Ladies and gentlemen, there won't be any upgrade – you came with just enough. Arise!

I think we are driven back from fulfilling our potential the more we look long at and ponder over negative circumstances – the absence/lack of physical, educational and economic infrastructure. We lose our grip on the situation the more we think the solution is 'out there'. The more we expect 'that someone' would come to our rescue the more we lose control. Look inwards. Look upwards. But not outward. It's in YOU. I choose to follow the advice from Norman Vincent Peale, "Become a possibilitarian. No matter how dark things seem to be or actually are, raise your sights and see possibilities – always see them, for they're always there".

Repeat this over and over for the next few days **"I am young, proud of it and taking my place"**.

Chapter Three

You were born for Excess!

**You were born
for Excess!**

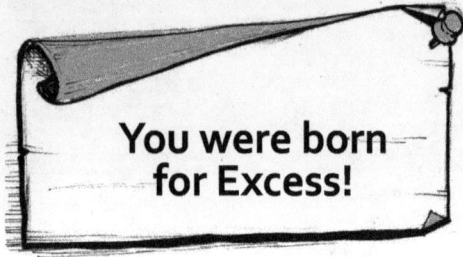

Our Deepest Fear

Our deepest fear is not that we are inadequate.
Our deepest fear is that we are powerful beyond
measure.

It is our light, not our darkness, that most frightens
us.
We ask ourselves, Who am I to be brilliant,
gorgeous, handsome, talented and fabulous?

Actually, who are you not to be?
You are a child of God.

Your playing small does not serve the world.
There is nothing enlightened about shrinking
so that other people won't feel insecure around you.
We are all meant to shine, as children do.

We were born to make manifest the glory of God
within us.
It is not just in some; it is in everyone.

And, as we let our own light shine, we consciously
give
other people permission to do the same.
As we are liberated from our fear,
our presence automatically liberates others.

Our Deepest Fear - excerpt from *A Return to Love*,
a book by motivational speaker and author
Marianne Williamson

Welcome to the day of Excess! Anything less would lead to sub-optimal living. Period! Excess is the only path to impact, contribution, and significance. Excess stands for any thought or deed that is considered excessive or unnecessary or out-of-order/hurried/ahead of its time. It represents an approach to life that seeks to conceive, envision, think and do beyond what is just sufficient or just required. Excess is a consciousness . . . a mindset that disbelieves a promissory future; disbelieves impossibilities and obstacles; and disbelieves established steps and norms.

Excess is unrestrained! Unrestrained by age, by country, by education, by money, etc. It is life without a leash! Truly free at last! Free to bring your best thought and your best effort. Free to create and invent - touching the ends of the earth with our ideas. Yes, our ideas. Bringing forth new possibilities just like those before us.

You were born (made) for this. This is what was said in the Book of Beginnings:"Then God said,   let us make man in our own image according to our likeness; let them have dominion over the fish of the sea, over the birds of the air, and over the cattle, over all the earth and over every creeping thing that creeps on the earth . . . Then God blessed them, and God said to them," *Be fruitful and multiply; fill the earth and subdue it; have dominion over the fish of the sea; over the birds of the air, and over every living thing that moves on the earth"*.[a]

Wow! Dominion over the earth! Fill the earth and subdue it? Now that's what I'm talking about – this is Excess to the nth degree!!! 'Fill', the last time I checked means: fill up, occupy, impart, pervade, saturate, spread through, encompass...It could mean like Myles Munroe who is filling up by being and doing several things (international minister, pastor, leadership expert and trainer, government adviser, businessman, best-selling author, etc)...Or could be Bill Gates who is spreading one big Microsoft into the corners of the earth and touching our lives in more ways everyday.

Subdue means to take control. Tame the earth. Calm

it down. Conquer the world! You are an overcomer. Overpower the earth. You are wired to win over your world. This is the day of Excess

Excess is blind disbelief of everything that holds true. If the Wright brothers had not disbelieved the world then, humankind would never have known air travel. Everything can be! At ages 32 and 36, Orville and Wilbur Wright conducted the first successful flight of a motor-powered airplane. Young people are free to choose and create.

Excess is a discomfort with established order or sequence. The most notable achievements, discoveries or inventions . . . the ones that have made generational impact were made by persons who defied one established order or the other. For example, what is common to all these people[b]:

> Bill Gates
> Roman Abramovich
> Andre Agassi
> Jane Austen
> Richard Branson
> Micheal Dell
> Charles Dickens
> Walt Disney
> Thomas Edison
> Larry Ellison

Henry Ford
J. B. Fuqua
J. Paul Getty
Abraham Lincoln
T. D. Jakes
Steve Jobs
Ingvar Kamprad
Ralph Lauren
Mike Lazaridis
John Major
David Ogilvy
Joel Osteen
George Orwell
Rosa Parks
Jay-Z
Mark Twain
Leon Uris
Mark Zuckerberg
Jerry Yang
John D. Rockefeller Sr
Cosmas Maduka
William Shakespeare
Anton van Leeuwenhoek

They dropped out of school/college/university or never even went to school. One of the most established order is that you must go to school. The established order is that you cannot start anything worthwhile if you have not gone to school. The established order is that you cannot be somebody unless you have gone to school. But these people were uncomfortable with the way things are done. They did not accept the excuse created by their circumstances. They were uncomfortable with what was acceptable. Break all rules! Young people are licensed to create new paths.

By the way who are these people who either dropped out of one school or didn't even go at all? Let me run through some of them for you:

Roman Abramovich, one time richest man in Russia, 107th richest man in the world, owner of the world's second largest yacht as at 2013 (533-foot *Eclipse*) and owner of Chelsea Football club. Dropped out of college. He studied at the Moscow State Auto Transport Institute before taking a leave of absence from academics to go into business. He later earned a correspondence degree from the Moscow State Law Academy.

Thomas Edison, multimillionaire inventor of the phonograph, light bulb, and many other inventions. Edison is the third most prolific inventor in history, holding 1,093 US patents in his name, as well as many patents in the United Kingdom, France, and Germany. He quit formal schooling after his teacher called him addled [*unable to think clearly, confused*].

Was home-schooled by his mother.

Mike Lazaridis, billionaire founder and co-CEO of Research in Motion (makers of *Blackberry* phones). At age 12, he won a prize at the Windsor Public Library for reading every science book in the library. "Two months before I graduated from college, I answered a request for proposal from General Motors with a five-page pitch to develop a network computer control display system. They offered me a half-million dollar contract.... I went to the president of the university to get his permission to take a leave of absence. He tried to persuade me to finish out my year, but when I told him about the contract, he wished me the best of luck." Since that time, he hasn't had time to go back and finish.

Walt Disney, producer, director, screenwriter, animator, developer of Disneyland. Winner of 26 Oscars and 7 Emmy awards. While attending McKinley High School, he also took night classes at the Chicago Art Institute. He dropped out of high school at the age of 16 to join the army. Rejected because he was under-aged, he joined the Red Cross and was sent to war in Europe. Upon his return from war, he began his artistic career.

Anton van Leeuwenhoek, microbiologist, microscope maker, and discoverer of bacteria, blood cells, and sperm cells. He is commonly known as "the

Father of Microbiology", and considered to be the first microbiologist. He also dropped out of high school.

Joel Osteen, best-selling author, senior pastor of the largest congregation in the US and host of the most-watched inspirational TV show in the U.S. Dropped out of Oral Roberts University after one year to care for his mother (who was recovering from cancer). His first book, *Your Best Life Now*, has sold more than 4 million copies.

Mark Zuckerberg, billionaire co-founder of Facebook, and the 66th richest person in the world (as at March 2013). Dropped out of Harvard to continue working on the social networking website he founded in his dorm room in 2004. Facebook has more than one billion users and a market capitalisation in excess of $58 billion as at May 2013. In 2010, Zuckerberg was named Time magazine's 'Person of the Year'.

Cosmas Maduka, CEO of Coscharis Group. The Coscharis Group of companies has at least eight subsidiaries. Cosmas lost his father at the age of four and as a result his education was cut short; at the age of seven he became an automobile apprentice in his uncle's automotive spare parts business in Lagos. He worked for his uncle for seven years before starting his own business in 1975. Cosmas' uncle provided him with N200 in capital with which he used to start his own auto parts business in Nnewi. In his biography, *From Trials to Triumph: The Coscharis Story*, he asks and answers the question: "Just how does one turn a 200 naira one-man business into a large conglomerate with over 15 billion naira in shareholders' funds in less than thirty years?"

The point isn't to suggest that people shouldn't go to school – far from it. The point is 1)the going to school sequence isn't the ONLY way to greatness; 2) the idea that all you have to do is go to school and everything would be great is a fallacy; 3) your certificate from school must not set the boundaries of your life; 4) be weary of your certificate robbing you of the ability to look inwards and ; 5) if you aren't currently able to go to school, move on and still maximize your life

Excess is firm belief in God and His gifts in each of us. *"What lies behind us and what lies before us are small matters compared to what lies within us. And when we bring what is within us out into the world, miracles happen"* - Ralph Waldo Emerson (American Essayist, Poet, 1803 – 1882). Or hear another *"Deep within man dwells those slumbering powers; powers that would astonish him, that he never dreamed of possessing; forces that would revolutionize his life if aroused and put into action"* - Orison Swett Marden (American Writer, Founder of Success Magazine, 1850-1924). Believe in YOU. Believe in God. As a young person, you have YOU as your greatest gift to humanity.

Excess is seeing possibilities. On the 28th of August 1963, a young man while addressing an American crowd of over 250,000 people made a speech in which he spoke of a world which far from existed. This is how that time was described, "In 1950's America, the equality of man envisioned by the Declaration of Independence was far from a reality. People of color — blacks, Hispanics, Asians — were discriminated against in many ways, both overt and covert". Yet a young man set out to envision and to speak of possibilities. That year that same man was named Man of the Year by Time magazine in 1963. The year after, the man would go down in history as the youngest person to ever receive a Nobel Prize for Peace at age 35.

The man is Martin Luther King Jnr. An excerpt from his famous *I Have a Dream* speech reads, "I have a dream that my four little children will one day live in a nation where they will not be judged by the color of their skin but by the content of their character. . . I have a dream that one day, down in Alabama, with its vicious racists, with its governor having his lips dripping with the words of interposition and nullification; one day right there in Alabama, little black boys and black girls will be able to join hands with little white boys and white girls as sisters and brothers". With God, all things really are possible. Young people are wired to see visions/dreams/possibilities.

Excess is relentless pursuit of excellence. Executing ideas with more care, thoughtfulness, and detail than is expected or required. A company and a CEO that epitomises excellence, likely more than most, is Apple* and its CEO, Steve Jobs. As at August 2012, Apple's market capitalization stood at an excess of $623 billion[c] making it the Most Valuable Public Company in history, a record previously held by Microsoft. It is the largest publicly traded company in the world, ahead of giants such as Microsoft, Shell and General Electric. It has held the award as the 'World's Most Admired Company' four years in a row – 2008, 2009, 2010 and 2011[d]

Hear the CEO, Steve Jobs: *"Be a yardstick of quality. Some people aren't used to an environment where excellence is expected." There is no shortcut to excellence. You will have to make the commitment to make excellence your priority. Use your talents, abilities, and skills in the best way possible and get ahead of others by giving that little extra. Live by a higher standard and pay attention to the details that really do make the difference. Excellence is not difficult – simply decide right now to give it your best shot – and you will be amazed with what life gives you back."[e]*

Apple* Inc. (previously Apple Computer Inc.) is an American multinational corporation that designs and markets consumer electronics, computer software, and

If you ask me, here is the Excellence master capsule: *"Excellence can be attained if you care more than others think is wise, risk more than others think is safe, dream more than others think is practical, and expect more than others think is possible."* – Author Anonymous. Pursue excellence!

Excess is doing the unnecessary. At different times the world or the people around you have j u d g e d   t h a t   s o m e t h i n g   i s unnecessary/pointless/needless. They either said the idea, product or service was unnecessary or the additions to the product or service were unnecessary. In essence they said it was worthless to go that route. Did you know that for a long time it was considered unnecessary for surgeons to wear clean gloves and wash their hands before and after operations? Now it seems commonsensical to expect them to have known but they didn't . . . and this would have remained so but for the work of Joseph Lister (1827-1912; Surgeon). It is recorded that "...many of his contemporaries laughed at him but Lister was said to have never bothered to reply and only heaved an occasional sigh at the world's stupidity."

---

personal computers. The company's best-known hardware products include the Macintosh line of computers, the iPod, the iPhone and the iPad. Apple software includes the Mac OS X operating system; the iTunesmedia browser; the iLife suite of multimedia and creativity software; the iWork suite of productivity software; Aperture, a professional photography package; Final Cut Studio, a suite of professional audio and film-industry software products; Logic Studio, a suitemusic production tools; and iOS, a mobile operating system.

The world has made long strides because some people chose to do the unnecessary. What separates the greats of our generation from the almost-great was the adventure into the unnecessary. Take the challenge today – venture down the path of the seemingly unnecessary. . . you never know what you may stumble upon.

Excess is massive effort. Doing more than is acceptable. It means instituting a series of massive actions. This is a lifestyle of deploying effort that is above and beyond what is satisfactory, conventional, customary, or adequate. 'Good enough' is never good enough - whatever your hand finds to do, do it with all your might (being the totality of your spiritual, mental, emotional and physical energy). Massive effort shows up in the quality (distinction or peculiarity) of the effort and also in the quantity (amount or volume). Anthony Robbins (*1960–present; Author, Speaker, Motivator*), as a teenager, read up to 700 books on human development, psychology, physiology, anything about thought within five years!

Arrive earlier even if they didn't say so. Wear your best clothes even if they didn't say so. Send in a well bound proposal even if they didn't say so. Come to the presentation with the whole of your team even if they didn't say so. Go ahead and check the venue days before the event, even if they didn't say so. Call 300 times if you have to. Send out more letters, resumes or proposals than anyone you have heard of. Ask if they were satisfied even if . . . Do much more today and . . . always. *"It is only through labour and painful effort, by grim energy and resolute courage, that we move on to better things"* - Theodore Roosevelt (26th President of the United States, 1858 – 1919).

Excess is Boundaryless. Touching corners of the earth with your ideas, products or solutions. Yes, you! There are no limits, no boundaries. Excess is to free your mind of all geographic limits and boundaries – your ideas, products and services can affect the way the world lives! That the world is a global village has been repeatedly proven by fortunate (Facebook) and unfortunate (global economic crunch) happenings. What started in the dormitory of one single college (Facebook, Harvard University) has permanently altered how we live. Greed and financial manipulations that started on a single street (Wall Street, United States) literally brought most of the world to its knees. The world is in need of your excess. Youth with their customary boundless energy and unconventional ideas are the world's last hope.

Excess is daring more. No one is going out on a limb anymore. "Be careful" seems to be the 'Advice of the Decade'. Living cautiously is a guaranteed route to sub-optimal living – it helps you accomplish not-a-thing. *"Refuse to join the cautious crowd that plays* *not to lose. Play to win"* – David Mahoney (Author). No one is taking risks anymore. We are in the day and age of 'calculated risks'. If it is calculated then I ask, "How can it be a risk?" *"Life is either a daring adventure, or nothing"* – Helen Keller (Author, Political activist, Lecturer, 1880–1968). Become known for doing what people said couldn't be done. Success always favours the gallant. Dare more, get on Excess-drive! Dare to go where you have never gone. Dare to do what you have never done. Dare to be who you have never being. Dare to start! **It is better to fail in doing something, than to excel in doing nothing**.

Look at what I stumbled on in John Mason's book; *Know Your Limits – Then Ignore them: "The courage to begin is the same courage it takes to succeed. This is the courage that usually separates dreamers from achievers. The beginning is the most important part of any endeavor. Worse than a quitter is anyone who is afraid to begin. Ninety percent of success is showing up and starting. You may be disappointed if you fail, but you are doomed if you don't try. . . to win, you must begin".*

Excess is Tenacity. The ability to stick to something until it produces the envisaged/desired result. Call it persistence, determination or grit if you like. People are so quick to throw in the towel these days. People give up too often and too soon. And young people are the worst offenders. I guess it's because we are in the

Blackberry era– instant messaging around the world in an instant.

We no longer hear of the person who
chose to wait for days before getting a
desired 10 minutes audience.
We no longer hear of the person who
decided to send 300 emails or letters
just to get another's attention.
We no longer hear of the person who
travelled for so many miles on a journey
that was an utter risk.
We no longer hear of the person who
was repeatedly turned down but kept
coming back.
We no longer hear of the person who
kept trying and trying ...
We no longer hear...
No longer. . .

Excess is youth. By physiological and spirituo-psychological design, youth is made for excess. By an inborn coding structure, young people want to go further, sooner, faster, etc. Young people, except where external circumstances have clipped their wings, are always on Excess-drive. No wonder the wise King Solomon said, *"The glory of young men is their strength..."*

Let me give you an example of another youth in excess (sit tight), the youngest person to have an office on Wall Street, New York and the youngest person conferred an Honorary Doctorate in HBCU history (HBCUs - Historically Black Colleges and Universities). Ladies and gentlemen, I present to you Dr. Farrah Gray.[f]

Timeline of Accomplishments

"My story, though unique, is not unlike others who began with nothing more than a dream fueled by sheer determination. I believe my story will remind you of the kid in all of us who knows no limits and believes anything – and everything – is possible." – Farrah Gray

Born September 9, 1984 and raised by a single mother in the inner city Chicago projects.

At Age 6,

⇒ Farrah Gray sold body lotion for $1.50 from door to door.

At Age 7,

⇒ He carried a business card that read "21st Century CEO".

At Age 8,

⇒ In Chicago, Farrah started UNEEC (Urban Neighborhood Economic Enterprise Club).

At Age 9,
⇒ At 9, almost 10, Farrah co-hosted radio show "Backstage Live" in Las Vegas reaching 12 million listeners every Saturday night.

At Age 12,
⇒ Farrah had a lucrative nationwide speaking career commanding $5,000 – $10,000 per appearance.

At Age 13,
⇒ Farrah started Farr-Out Foods, a specialty foods company headquartered in New York, targeting young people.

At Age 14,
⇒ Farrah officially became a millionaire by hitting sales of $1.5 million for Farr-Out Foods.
⇒ Farrah started New Early Entrepreneur Wonders (NE2W) Student Venture Fund.

At Age 15,
⇒ Farrah acquired *INNERCITY* Magazine from Inner City Broadcasting Corporation.

At Age 17,
⇒ Farrah financed a comedy show on the Las Vegas Strip, which gave him the distinct honor of being the second African-American after Red Foxx to own a show production on the Las Vegas strip.

At Age 19,

⇒ Farrah signed his *"Reallionaire"* book deal with HCI.

⇒ Farrah Gray became a contributing author to*"Chicken Soup for the African-American Soul"*. Both books were published by Health Communications Incorporated (HCI) publisher of the *New York Times* and *USA Today* best-seller *Chicken Soup for the Soul* series.

At Age 20,

⇒ Farrah, as a real estate investor, was elected as youngest member to sit on the Board of Directors of the National Association of Real Estate Brokers, Inc. Region 15 (N.A.R.E.B.®), the oldest and largest minority trade association.

⇒ Became an international best-selling author with the book *Reallionaire*.

At Age 21,

⇒ Became Spokesman for the National Coalition for the Homeless.

⇒ First Premiere Bank released the "GoFarr" Farrah Gray Mastercard.

⇒ Launched University of Business Futures (UBF), an entrepreneurship school, developed in a partnership with the Ewing Marion Kauffman Foundation and graduated with 300 students (at inception).

⇒ Became the youngest in HBCU history to receive an honorary doctorate from Allen University.

At Age 22,
⇒ Co-founded Realty Pros a property asset management company.
⇒ Became Spokesman for National Marrow Donor Program African-American Initiative.
⇒ Became a syndicated columnist through the National Newspapers Publishers Association (NNPA), a federation of 200 weekly newspapers, reaching over 15 million readers.
⇒ Became an AOL Money Coach.

At Age 23,
⇒ Released the *"Get Real, Get Rich: Conquer the 7 Lies Blocking You from Success"* (Dutton Hardcover) and Brilliance Audio Book on CD, Cassette, MP3 CD

At Age 24,
⇒ Realty Pros reached over $30 million in total assets under management.
⇒ Serving second term as Chairman of The National Coalition for the Homeless Bringing America Home Campaign.
⇒ Released *"The Truth Shall Make You Rich: The New Road Map to Radical Prosperity"* (Plume Paperback). Gray's books have been translated into Russian, Korean, Indonesian and Vietnamese languages with book sales in Africa, Australia, Europe and in Central and South American countries.

At Age 25,

⇒ Farrah Gray Publishing (FGP), book publishing house launched and distributed by HCI Books, which published the world famous #1 New York Times, USA Today and Guinness Book of World Records, best-selling Chicken Soup for the Soul series. *Chicken Soup for the Soul* has sold more than 112 million copies, with titles translated into more than 40 languages and total retail sales of *Chicken Soup for the Soul* branded merchandise have topped $1.3 billion.

⇒ CNN "Up from the Past: African-American Firsts" featured as an American trailblazer, extraordinary entrepreneur.

⇒ Named as one of the "20 Modern History Makers" in the 20th Anniversary issue of Upscale Magazine.

⇒ Recognized as a "Living Legend" Who's Who In Black Las Vegas.

At Age 26,

⇒ 2010 Trumpet Award Young Entrepreneur Recipient

⇒ Released first title of Farrah Gray Publishing (FGP), *Dear Dad* by the son of legendary Reggae icon Bob Marley, Ky-Mani Marley

⇒ Named to the inaugural list of Chicago's The Urban Business Roundtable's "Top 40 Game-

Changers" as entrepreneurial prodigy.

⇒ Received the 24th Annual 100 Black Men of America, Inc. Conference Award.

⇒ Honored by City of Louisville, Kentucky Dr. Farrah Gray Day Proclamation.

Chapter Four

**Nothing has succeeded
as Excess!**

Nothing has succeeded as Excess!

*"Moderation is a fatal thing.
Nothing succeeds like excess"*

- Oscar Wilde
(Irish Dramatist, Novelist, Poet; 1854-1900)

There are a lot of success stories and yours is been written already. But a lot of people, organizations and even nations have stumbled on success/greatness by doing the seemingly unnecessary. There is a new reality and we have to awaken to it. We are now in the world of wants and not needs. The lines between needs and wants have become blurred. What people want has become a need. No longer must things make practical sense. I am not advocating that things shouldn't make sense. Organizations must continue to seek ways to add value to people. Your survival depends on your

ability to add value to people, but your greatness may depend on more than that. Remember that value is in the eye of the beholder. What I am simply saying is that the limits/boundaries of value have been extended by the consumer. . . extended to include emotional and social appeal. I'll give you examples.

Was it necessary?

Facebook. Facebook has more than one billion active users (as at September 2012) – six times the size of Nigeria put together and inching closer to the size of China (>1.3 billion people) every passing day. The company's market capitalisation is valued in excess of $58 billion as at May 2013[a]. **But was Facebook necessary?** Is it necessary now as well? Is our life incomplete without it? Was it discovered after an all-weekend strategy session by a group of professors seeking for ways to add value to our world? Nope. A young undergraduate stumbled on the idea while looking for ways by which students could rate the faces (pictures) of their colleagues over the internet. "According to *The Harvard Crimson*, the site was comparable to *Hot or Not*, and "used photos compiled from the online facebooks of nine houses, placing two next to each other at a time and asking users to choose the 'hotter' person". That is why it is an internet based 'book' of faces (pictures) – facebook. What may have been considered unnecessary has entirely changed the way we live, employs over 4,900 staff and has given us two of the youngest billionaires yet – the 2013 Youngest Billionaire (Dustin Moskovitz*) and CEO, Mark Zuckerberg.

GTBank. Won the award as the most profitable bank in Nigeria as at May 2013[b]. When the bank started in 1990, it was received as a necessary and desired bank by the consumer. For it arrived at a time when it was customary to spend long hours in the bank, just waiting to collect money. This waiting time virtually disappeared with its arrival and that of its peers. But was it necessary to have chandeliers in the banking hall when it started? Was it necessary to have a piano playing within the bank? Were they mandated to declare a loss when they could have waited and declared a profit? Was it required in banking to have paintings on the wall? Maybe what was unnecessary is what granted them access into the hearts and minds of Nigerians and now the world. Maybe?

---

*The world's youngest billionaire, Dustin Moskovitz, was Mark Zuckerberg's Harvard roommate and Facebook's third employee. His net worth is $3.8billion according to 2013 Forbes report. He is just eight days younger than his friend (both 26years as at 2011). The two dropped out of Harvard and moved to California to work for the social networking firm full time; he was its first chief technology officer and then vice president of engineering. He left in 2008 to start Asana, a software company that allows individuals and small companies to better collaborate. Values of his new company: "pragmatism," "being a mensch," "admitting when you're wrong" and "chill-ness." Source: forbes.com

Daystar. Stands as one of Nigeria's most impactful churches. Yes, it is desirable that we have churches where the Bible and its impact on our daily choices and our community are taught. It is also desirable for the church to provide parking lots (all organisations in fact) for their parishioners. But was it necessary to provide air-conditioned buses to convey them from the car lot to the church and back? A distance of just about a 100metres? I didn't think so at that time and I voiced my misgivings. I simply said to myself that this was unnecessary. Then they took their time and installed air conditioners within the auditorium. And this was at a time when places their size had only bothered to install fans. What about them having all the restrooms installed with air conditioners? So were these developments necessary? My answer now? Yes. Yes. Yes. Haven't we gotten too accustomed to mistreating or under-treating ourselves? The seemingly unnecessary can become the functional – it's just a matter of time.

Globacom. The man who sits on top of this Nigerian-based telecommunications company at the time of its inception/birth also sat on two banks, an oil company and other trading concerns. So was it necessary for him to bid for the license to own a telecoms firm? Wasn't he rich already? He certainly was. Should he even have bidded, particularly after losing money in the first bidding round some years earlier? But he did. What he got himself into is now arguably the largest telecommunications company in Nigeria. Granting him (Mike Adenuga), access into a truly global industry with room for growth; access into a cash-spinning retail business; and access finally into the list of the world's richest people[c]. The venture into Excess could just be the differentiator between local and international success.

Harry Porter. By the time the Harry Porter fantasy books arrived didn't we have enough story books already? Were we lacking in fictional stories? No, we were doing just fine. The book was submitted to twelve publishing houses, all of which rejected the manuscript! Then the books came, one more title after another. Crowds began to line up to buy on launch day – more than 400 million copies sold to date! Movies made from the books followed with resounding success as well. The writer (J. K. Rowling) became the 12th richest woman in Great Britain, progressing from living on benefits to multi-millionaire status within five years for an idea she conceived in 1990[d]. Maybe sometimes what appears to be unnecessary can actually in some cases become more successful than its predecessors. I am even working on a theory now that there is no saturated market anywhere.

iPad. I can understand the usefulness of the ipod (you can hold more music with you in a very small container). Good and very functional and it was a hit(still is). But this thing called the iPad – is it necessary? We already have phones, computers, laptops/notebooks, and even netbooks. Conclusion: the iPad is unnecessary. Simple. However, follow this: on the day of its launch in the US they sold more than 300,000 units. Two years after, not only have they sold over 19 million units (as at March 2011) but they have *'inspired'* other companies to produce their own versions: Playbook, Galaxy, Xoom, Streak, Cius, Slate, Kindle Fire HD etc (there are more than 20 variants of the iPad by other companies). The manufacturer's (Apple) market capitalization increases and it retains its spot as the Most Admired Company in the world. Wait for this: we woke up one day and iPad 2 is live! Then even iPad 3. This product would easily win the award as the *'most wanted seemingly unnecessary'* product. By 2012, it has sold over 100 million pieces. Maybe we have many yet undiscovered wants in the human race. What the people want, the people don't know. Your task is to help them uncover it – just like Apple.

Going to the moon. I can understand the value in air travel – saves time and is comfortable. Period. But going to the moon! Com'on. Was it necessary then and is it necessary now? My answer is a resounding "No"? But didn't God say "fill and subdue"? And that is exactly what landing a man on the moon is all about. What do they stand to gain? I honestly don't have all the answers, but I'll tell you something in a whisper. Every time a spaceship landed on the moon and completed its mission successfully, Man pushed further the limits of human achievement. And you and I never know what we can find on the outer limits of human possibilities.

Name other examples . . .

What else would we find if we pursued those things that the world around or the people around us have labeled as unnecessary, needless or excessive? Remember that what was once said to be unnecessary proved later to be exactly what people wanted. What was labeled at one time excessive has also been found to unearth unexpressed yearnings in people. Sometimes they say it is pointless getting into that venture because a lot of people are already into it. In other cases, everyone agrees that it is an avoidable product/service/project, but everyone would be buying it. Or some other *'unnecessaries'* just beat our mind . . . stretch our imaginations . . . produce a certain experience. . . a feeling . . . an elixir.

Your survival depends on your ability to add functional value to people. But greatness may rest on your capacity to take people through an adventure into the *'unnecessary'* . . . into Excess.

Chapter Five

Make Over-Do your strategy

Make Over-Do your strategy

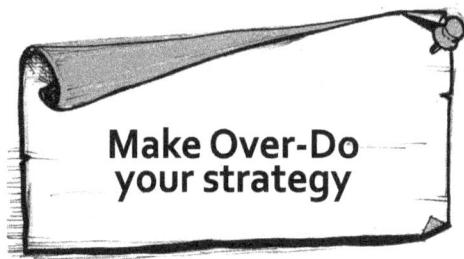

"Carpe Diem! Seize the day.
Make your lives extraordinary."

– Movie (*Dead Poet's Society*)

Obviously, we would need to make huge amendments in the way we have lived our lives – if we are to make meaning of it . . . if we are to make the most of it . . . and if we are to maximize it. Our story shouldn't be described by this quote, *"I have spent my days stringing and unstringing my instrument, while the song I came to sing remains unsung".* – Tagore

Cultivate blind disbelief for everything that holds true. Whatever they say cannot be done – doubt it immediately. Whatever they say is not being done, jump at it and do it. If they say that *'people don't do it that way'*, go ahead and do it anyway. In the next few days find something to think and to do that defies the norm. Whatever has become normal is the least that is possible – whatever hasn't yet existed may be the most that is attainable.

Beat the Sequence. Look for a sequence in life that you can beat. If you do, you just may be on to something that no one in your lineage has done before. There is no process that is cast in stone. At work, in school or at play (yes at play), seek for ways to make things shorter, faster, cheaper, or more convenient. Or just create a new way entirely. Break down every rule. Did you hear me? I said break down every rule. Do not let any rule be the explanation for your delay.

Become Known for Doing. Guess what? There are too many people talking and nobody is doing. Become known for doing. One of the best advice ever given to young people by any organization, is this one by Nike: "Just do it"! No one ever gets a price for what *'she was planning to do'*. The world has been known to applaud courageous attempts. It is great to come 1st, 2nd or 3rd but even participants get their names mentioned, their photographs taken and sometimes a prize. No one gives a prize or mentions the names of the people at home who *'feel'* that they are better and that they could have won. Get out of the house and participate – just do it. This advice is one of the most daring advice ever given by anyone (call it Excess): *"Anything worth doing is worth doing badly."* – Gilbert Chesterton (1874-1936, writer, poet).

"It is not the critic who counts, not the man who points out how the strong man stumbled, or where the doer of deeds could have done better. The credit belongs to the man who is actually in the arena, whose face is marred by dust and sweat and blood, who strives valiantly, who errs and comes short again and again, who knows the great enthusiasms, the great devotions, and spends himself in a worthy cause, who at best knows achievement and who at the worst, if he fails, at least fails while daring greatly so that his place shall never be with those cold and timid souls who know neither victory nor defeat" – Theodore Roosevelt. Selah!

Carpe Diem! Seize the Day! Ladies and gentlemen, NOW is a gift – use it. *"Warning: Dates on the calendar are closer than they appear"* – Author unknown. There are too many procrastinators around town. As much as it depends on you, get OUT of their midst right Now! Do whatever you can immediately. Make *'carpe diem'* your default setting. Yes, there would still be some things that have to wait but when it is your default setting to seize every opportunity that comes you would miss fewer ones. *"Small opportunities are often the beginning of great enterprises."* - Demosthenes (Greek statesman, orator, 384–322 BC). Miracles reside in almost every opportunity that is seized. Seize today and don't postpone till tomorrow. *"Seize the day, and put the least possible*

trust in tomorrow" – Horace (65 – 8BC, poet).

Make excess your core value. Make it your life's goal to use every gift or talent or strength that you have right where you are. Accept no excuses, however real, however true. Don't be the provider and protector of excuses. Subdue your environment where you are right now. Take charge of things in your neighbourhood, class, or school (primary, secondary, polytechnic, college of education, nursing, university, craft, tailoring, mechanic workshop, saloon, anywhere). Make it your responsibility to bring out your best and the best in others. Do it faster, easier, more creative than before. Add MORE cubes to every endeavour that you are cooking. And require that of people around you as well. Let your group/club be known for excellence.   Let people always expect that you would put in the better effort. Make over-do your strategy. Become known for doing MORE than is requested, demanded, or expected.

Cause something to happen or exist because of you. In the next three months (at the most), cause something to happen. Or cause something to exist because of you. Get it? If people join you fine, if they don't some others will. Just start something. It doesn't have to 'look' big in the beginning. It could be a business, a group, a cause, a class, a task, a project whatever – cause something to happen right away. Start a fire!

Never Say Never. In Excess school, one of the first things you learn is that failure is not permanent until you say so. You are not your failure – the fact that you failed at something in one or two or three or four or five or six or seven or eight or nine or . . . attempts doesn't make you a failure. You must NEVER define yourself by your performance. What if it was just a bad day? Don't let a temporary setback become your set back. Keep on keeping on. Listen to this advice given by a 17 year old:

"See, I never thought that I could walk through fire.
I never thought that I could take the burn.
I never had the strength to take it higher,
Until I reached the point of no return.
And there's just no turning back,
When your heart's under attack,
Gonna give everything I have,
It's my destiny.
I will never say never! (I will fight)
I will fight till forever! (make it right)
Whenever you knock me down,
I will not stay on the ground.
Pick it up,
Pick it up,
Pick it up,
Pick it up up up,
And never say never. . ."
- part of lyrics from Justin Bieber's song,
Never Say Never

"Success is a function of persistence and doggedness and the willingness to work for twenty-two minutes to make sense of something that most people would give up on after thirty seconds" – Malcolm Gladwell, *The Outliers*

Out-learn. Read up beyond what is required of you right now. Know more than is expected of you right now. Learn more than is demanded in your circumstances. Over-do it. We didn't say you should brag about it. All we are saying is "arm yourself with knowledge" 'cos you would need it down the road. Read up. Read often. Read wide.

Doubt your fears. Doubt every fear that you have. Starve your fears by doing and by affirmations. Say with me, "I can do it". Don't organize pity parties for yourself. Don't seek for sympathizers. No one was born with a fear – we learn to fear as we go along.

Divorce yourself from your circumstances. Please do not give honorary titles to your circumstances. Don't make your situation 'special'. 'Cos you are going thru' the same things others are going thru' or others have gone thru'. You either get through it or you are through. You didn't create your circumstances; you only found yourself in it so don't say "if only they knew what I was going through". Even if you created it "I also do not condemn you, go and sin no more" is what the Lord says. Do you desire new circumstances? Then accept that things can change right now. Embrace the change in your heart right now. Envision the change in your mind's eye. Take bold steps now. Make a decision right now. *"Decision determines destiny"* - Anthony Robbins.

Put pressure on your strengths and skills. You have one life to live – please live it. Live it every second, every hour and every day. How? Put pressure on your strengths/talents and skills. Spend your strengths and skills for the good of humankind every day from whatever age. Don't wait to perfect it, for it perfects itself from every use. So use it. Practice makes better, more practice makes much better, lots of early-years deliberate practice makes great. Find or create every and any avenue to expend your strengths/talents and skills. Volunteer your strengths and skills. Don't join the greats that we never heard of. *"Many great athletes are legendary for the brutal discipline of their practice routines. In basketball, Michael Jordan practiced intensely beyond the already punishing team practices"* – Geoffrey Colvin (thinker, editor Fortune).

Associate Higher. Get mentors. People who have attained or conquered some of the ground that you are yet to conquer. Listen to them and learn from them. One thing you are guaranteed is that you won't make the same mistakes that they made. You can have a mentor in more than one area. Remember though that no mentor is perfect. We are ALL work-in-progress. You can get a mentor through the person's books and tapes. This means you would devotedly read everything (as much as possible) written by the person. If John C. Maxwell is your mentor – you better hurry up with the reading. I am not saying you can't learn from your present group of friends but someone made this point the other day: *"friends are like the button on an elevator, they either take you up or down"*. Associate in the direction that you are going and not necessarily where you are now. This is one of the ways to permanently get a divorce from your circumstances.

Put in loads of Hardwork. Roll up your sleeves and get some work done. Sorry, there are no awards for laziness. Give whatever it takes to get a great job done. Learn this art at an early age and you have secured a future for yourself. Putting in quality effort has nothing to do with being rich or seemingly less privileged. *"Success is a ladder you cannot climb with your hands in your pockets"* – American Proverb

Read the gist below, excerpted from an article by an editor at Fortune, Geoffrey Colvin, titled "What it takes to be great" [a].

> *"Research now shows that the lack of natural talent is irrelevant to great success. The secret? Painful and demanding practice and hard work ... The first major conclusion is that nobody is great without work. It's nice to believe that*

if you find the field where you're naturally gifted, you'll be great from day one, but it doesn't happen. There's no evidence of high-level performance without experience or practice.

Reinforcing that no-free-lunch finding is vast evidence that even the most accomplished people need around ten years of hard work before becoming world-class, a pattern so well established researchers call it the ten-year rule.

What about Bobby Fischer, who became a chess grandmaster at 16? Turns out the rule holds: He'd had nine years of intensive study . . .So greatness isn't handed to anyone; it requires a lot of hard work. Yet that isn't enough, since many people work hard for decades without approaching greatness or even getting significantly better. What's missing? Practice makes perfect. The best people in any field are those who devote the most hours to what the researchers call "deliberate practice." – i.e activity that's explicitly intended to improve performance, that reaches for objectives just beyond one's level of competence, provides feedback on results and involves high levels of repetition".

Your age is good enough. Never ever allow the thought that you are too young for something settle in your mind. So when do you think that you would be old enough? You would never know unless you try. *"Sometimes age succeeds, sometimes it fails. It depends on you"* – Ravensara Noite. *"The young, free to act on their initiative, can lead their elders in the direction of the unknown... the children, the young, must ask the questions that we would never think to ask, but enough trust must be re-established so that the elders will be permitted to work with them on the answers."* - Margaret Mead (anthropologist, writer, 1901-1978).

I still can't get over the news that a teenager, with barely three years of public singing experience (discovered in 2008, debut single in 2009 – do the Maths), would even dare come near any of Micheal *'The Legend'* Jackson's achievements. It is now official, the Justin Bieber's musical documentary film *Never Say Never* has surpassed Michael Jackson's *This Is It* in American box office revenue! and has been dubbed the 'Third-Highest-Grossing Documentary of All Time'[b].

Experiment with everything. Develop a curiosity to test everything. "I would attempt it" are the first steps towards greatness. Fan your curiosity regularly – try out something new. Experiment because you never know where it could lead to. *What if* it comes out well? You may say what if it turns out badly? The lessons you learn from experience prepare you for the next platform of your life. It was Justin Bieber's mum, Mallette, that just kept uploading her son's small-time videos on Youtube and that is how someone saw it and tracked him down in Canada and the rest is history. Make that move today, because *what if...*

Put pressure on God. Wake up every day knowing and expecting that God is at work on your behalf. Be expectant. Believe that God loves you and cares about you. And while you are at it, never rate God by your circumstances. So if you get a candy, then God is good. If you don't have money in your pocket then God must be on holiday. Don't be like those wimpy children. As far as the sun remains, expect God to be working out the best in and through you. *"For I know the thoughts that I think toward you, says the LORD, thoughts of peace and not of evil, to give you a future and a hope"*[c] .

. . . .

FYI, the best days of your life starts now.

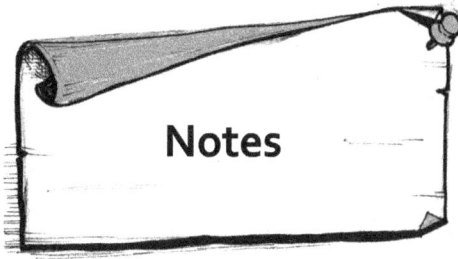

Notes

Introduction
(pg - XXI)

Information regarding Oscar Pristorius was gotten from the web and television. His story is compiled together here as an example and not an indication of endorsement or participation.
http://www.boocelebs.co.za/sport_oscar.htm
http://www.guardian.co.uk/sport/2011/aug/29/osc ar-pistorius-400m-final
http://www.ossur.com/
www.wikipedia.com

Chapter 1:
It is late for Smallness! ---------- (pg- 1)

[a]Poverty line - The poverty threshold, or poverty line, is the minimum level of income deemed necessary to achieve an adequate standard of living in a given country. In practice, like the definition of poverty, the official or common understanding of the poverty line is significantly higher in developed countries

than in developing countries. The common international poverty line has in the past been roughly $1 a day. In 2008, the World Bank came out with a revised figure of $1.25 at 2005 purchasing-power parity. Source: Wikipedia.com. Nigeria poverty line is available on www.cia.gov

Chapter 2:
Youth and Singleness:
A badly defined brand---------(pg - 10)

[a] Inventions that changed the way we live - www.greenspaceslandscaping.com

[b] Information regarding these individuals was all gotten from the web and books. Their names and part of their stories are mentioned as examples and not intended to imply their endorsement or participation.

Ultimate Business Resource, 2003. *Movers and Shakers: The 100 Most Influential Figures in Modern Business*, Cambridge, USA, Basic Books

Chapter 3:
You were born for Excess-------(pg - 35)

[a] Genesis 1: 26 & 28 – vs 26 "Then God said, "Let Us make man in Our image, according to Our likeness; let them have dominion over the fish of the sea, over the birds of the air , and over the cattle, over all the earth and over every creeping thing that creeps on

the earth." vs 28 "Then God blessed them, and God said to them, "Be fruitful and multiply; fill the earth and subdue it; have dominion over the fish of the sea, over the birds of the air, and over every living thing that moves on the earth." (New King James Bible)

[b]Information regarding these individuals was also gotten from the web and books. Their names and part of their stories are mentioned as examples and not intended to imply their endorsement or participation.

College Dropouts Hall of Fame - http://www.collegedropoutshalloffame.com/

The Bloomberg ranking of CEO undergraduate alma maters shows corporate chieftains come from across the country - http://www.businessweek.com/magazine/content/10_21/b4179020050124.htm

[c]Market capitalisation (often called market cap) is a measurement of size of a business enterprise (corporation) equal to the share price times the number of shares outstanding (shares that have been authorized, issued, and purchased by investors) of a publicly traded company. As owning stock represents ownership of the company, including all its equity, capitalization could represent the public opinion of a company's net worth and is a determining factor in stock valuation. Source wikipedia.com.

Apple Incorporated's market capitalisation stood at an excess of $623 billion at August 2012, according to www.finance.yahoo.com

"As Apple's stock rose to new high on Monday, the technology giant set another record: It became the most valuable public company in history. Apple's market value - the price of its stock multiplied by the number of outstanding shares - soared to $623.5 billion at the market's close. That eclipsed the previous record of $618.9 billion set by Microsoft on Dec. 30, 1999, at the height of the dot-com bubble..."- www.money.cnn.com, August 20, 2012

[d]Yearly Most Admired Company rankings by Forbes on www.money.cnn.com

[e]10 Golden Lessons from Steve Jobs-Ririan Project - http://ririanproject.com/2007/04/20/10-golden-lessons-from-steve-jobs/

[f]The story of Farrah Gary is presented here also as an example and not an indication of endorsement or participation.

Farrah, G, 2004 . *Reallionaire: Nine Steps to Becoming Rich from the Inside Out*, Benin, Nigeria, Joint Heirs

http://makelifeepic.wordpress.com/2010/12/16/spotlight-dr-farrah-gray-millionaire-mogul-at-age-14/

http://www.drfarrahgray.com/

Chapter 4:
Nothing has succeeded as Excess--(pg 59)

[a]Facebook's market capitalisation as at May 2013 was in excess of $58.78 billion. www.bloomberg.com and www.wikinvest.com

As at January 2011, Facebook was reportedly worth over $50billion - Goldman Sachs and Facebook had reportedly landed a $500 million investment from Goldman Sachs (GS) and a Russian investor that placed a $50 billion implied price tag on the social-networking giant. According to The New York Times, Wall Street titan Goldman and Russian investment firm Digital Sky Technologies invested $450 million and $50 million, respectively. Source: dealbook.nytimes.com

www.mashable.com

[b]GTBank – from www.gtbank.com

[c]Mike Adenuga – Forbes list of Richest people.

[d]J. K. Rowling - http://news.scotsman.com/ and http://www.jkrowling.com/textonly/en/

Chapter 5:
Make Over-do your strategy-----(pg 68)

[a] What it takes to be great -
http://money.cnn.com/magazines/fortune/fortune_archive/2006/10/30/8391794/index.htm

[b] Justin Bieber's musical documentary film *Never Say Never* has surpassed Michael Jackson's *This Is It* in US box office revenue
http://www.mtv.com/news/articles/1659185/justin-bieber-never-say-never-box-office.jhtml

http://thecelebritycafe.com/feature/justin-bieber-breaks-michael-jacksons-box-office-record-03-21-2011

[c] Jeremiah 29:11, New King James version of the Bible